Viriditas

Medha Pandey

BookLeaf
Publishing

India | USA | UK

Presentation by *BookLeaf Publishing*

Web: www.bookleafpub.com

E-mail: info@bookleafpub.com

ISBN: 9789363314894

First edition 2024

DEDICATION

Dedicated to the lotus feet of my Gurus including my first Guru - my mother.

Thank you for your all encompassing embrace, your never ending grace and your enlightening guidance.

I can never thank you enough.

Seeking your blessings, always.

ACKNOWLEDGEMENT

I am profoundly grateful to my family, whose unwavering support has been the cornerstone of my journey in crafting this collection of poems. To my parents and my elder sister, your love, encouragement, and understanding have fueled my creative spirit and inspired me to delve deeper into the realms of poetry. A special mention goes to my niece Ananya, whose infectious laughter and playful spirit never fail to bring out the child in me, infusing joy into every word penned.

I extend my heartfelt appreciation to Sadhguru for illuminating my path and enriching my soul. Additionally, I express my deep gratitude to my mentor, Aaron, whose insightful counsel and friendship have broadened my professional perspective and challenged me to see the world through new eyes. To all my friends who have stood by me with unwavering support and encouragement, thank you for being the pillars of my strength during this journey as a poet.

PREFACE

In the pages of this collection, you will embark on a journey through the intricacies of the human experience, as seen through the eyes of the poetess. These verses are a reflection of the myriad emotions, thoughts, and moments that have woven themselves into the fabric of her existence.

Drawing inspiration from her various real-life experiences and her fantasies, these poems resonate with the vibrancy and diversity of the world around us. They speak not only to those who seek solace in poetry but also to the youth who are curious, well-read, and curious about a multitude of subjects.

As you journey through the pages, you will encounter moments of joy, sorrow, wonder, and contemplation—each poem, a snapshot of a fleeting emotion or an idea captured in time. Through the lens of her perspective, you are invited to see the world anew, to find beauty in the mundane, and to embrace the complexities that make us human. May you find your destination during this journey!

My Guru

"Who is he?" I asked as a young chap
"He's Sadhguru beta!" My dad replies

As he talks about the ashram and the initiation
and the man, the miracle-oh my imagination!

Dad's just getting old I think

My sister jumps on the bandwagon in the US
Really? I think to myself, it can't possibly be
THAT big a deal

As the YouTube videos and books find their way
into my lap
The longing to know it all, oh the gap!!

"Who is he?" A friend asks looking at the book
"Oh that's Sadhguru" I replied

As days turn to months turn to years…..
Reality turns worse than some of my fears

Health takes a dip and emotions take a fall
Growing up is a tough task after all :)

"Who is he?" I thought to myself
"He's your guru" my heart replied

There's no way! I'm just 30!

The mind too stupid to comprehend and the
heart too full to receive
I continue to run away, to self-deceive

And one day I'm caught in a land of the
stranges….in my dreams…where suffering
doesn't follow any ranges!
Alone at home in the middle of the
night….despair, nosebleeds, sheer fright!

A figure appears, in silhouette and calls my
name
Brings me back to my senses, back to the reality
frame

I saw him? it was just a dream….I thought to
myself
When the 'Grace of Yoga' notification lit my
phone up on the shelf

I arrived in the middle of the heaven
With Dhyanlingam and Linga Bhairavi by his
side, he stood right there in front of my eyes

As tears rolled down I knew not why
But I knew that the darkness in my heart needed
this light

The year passed and the mandalas poured in
Bhuta shudhi, jalaneti, hatha yoga and inner
engineering

Kashi krama and marghazi…what's that? Oh
well, these experiences must be had!

"Can he fulfill my wishes?!" A young nephew
chimes
"I don't know child, I'm too drunk on the
divine"

"Medha, You're really not coming to Goa for
new years?! I booked flights…" my best friend
asks, surprised

"I'll be with him"
"Who is he?" She sighed

"My everything..my Guru"

I joyfully replied

Bitch

oh her?! she is a bitch

why ? she is fierce like a tigress
and is not afraid
of showing her prowess
so, she is a bitch

why? she speaks her mind
even if disliked
how arrogant of her, they find
so, she is a bitch

why? she takes up space
does not shrink her presence
makes eye contact in their face
so, she is a bitch

why? her character does not waver
refuses their coffee & dinner
she knows it is either to flirt or to curry her favor
so, she is a bitch

why? make their eyes twitch
let them see defeat, how they couldn't tame her!
their hearts burn and their brains itch
so girl, go on .. be a proud bitch :)

Freedom

I am free to do as I please….

Free to go out, chase the sunlight
Befriend the mountains, engage in some
streamside play
Let the sand get stuck in my hair; wet from the
salt and the sea
Go pet the strays and dance in the rain
Meet complete strangers over a cup of sizzling
coffee while taking shelter from the hail

But a passing thought brings me worry, why
does everyone else seem to be in a hurry?
Settling down, buying dwellings, having a
soulmate by their side and hugging their darlings
Little kids causing a chaos, dogs cats and
bunnies to take care of
What am I missing? Should I be on this path
too?
Eh, I just set sail…..”onto the next!” I yell

Freely sitting on my office desk, toiling away
Waiting for the next big thing, big project, raise,
promotion, the whole array
The bell of disquiet and unease takes a toll

Colleagues having pictures of their loved ones as
desk decorations
Talking about romantic vacations and wedding
celebrations!
What am I missing? Should I be on this path
too?

Free to go out and meet the potential suitors
The rap artists, the finance professionals, and the
coaches and tutors
Spend the evening, see the sun set
Forgive the past lovers and forget
With a big smile on my face

Pondering over the state of my heart
Trying to perfect this courting art
The thoughts keep piling up
Is it my time to settle down?
Enough of the society's frown

Explaining why I deserve a man who gets me
Why my career fulfils me
Why the thought of being a mother does not
seem to be

Because as I discovered

True freedom is the freedom to break free from
my own train of thoughts

Free from the shackles of the society and its
image of ifs and oughts'
From the expectations and burdens of how you
are viewed

True freedom is to move towards your innermost
core and nature
Only then will this constant comparison seize
Because I am the new age woman

And I am free to do as I please….

Healing

We too shall heal

Slowly but surely,
There will come a day when we are not the first
thought in each other's mind in the morning
Nor the last cry before hitting the bed for sleep
No vivid dreams, No fears or apprehensions
The mind too busy to overthink and the heart too
full to feel
Slowly but surely…

One day, soon enough,
The bright highlight of your DP will not send me
into a frenzy
Desperately looking for your name in the list of
'people who viewed your story' shall cease
Talking about you with friends and well-wishers
won't be trendy,
Will cease to garner any sympathy

One day, My eyes will not search for you in
every event that I attend
We will not try to attract each others' attention
by posting thirst trap reels

We will not actively try to get info on one
another with the same zeal

Soon, our mutual friends will reveal
That we indeed have found new romantic
interests
That we are going around doing the same things
that we used to do together, with someone we
just met
They won't be concerned with how we deal

For when we 'move on' for the world, with
smiles on our faces and new lovers in our arms
Lots of work and newfound charms
We will be turning the wheel

My love, that day,
We too shall heal

Empowerment

It is now time to empower our men.

Yes, you read that right.

It is time we took a stand to protect our culture
and civilization,
From sure shot ruin or worse, annihilation

Not telling boys to be strong & to cull their
negative emotions
Not force fitting into a glass their personalities'
ocean

Not glamourizing (child) sexual assault by older
women as a 'win'
Not mocking them for being obese, too muscular
or too thin

Not forcing them to glutton substances way
before the legal age limit
Not making their mistakes as talk of the town
turning into an exhibit

Not taking away their hobbies and interests for
being lady-like

Not coercing them to just play sports…….bike
& hike

Helping them to express their needs, wants and
challenges
Telling them that they can be different, yet
talented

Not taking away their childhood in the name of
being tough
Allowing them to draw boundaries when enough
is enough

Teaching them to love and grieve freely,
irrespective of what people say
Being their support group so they can handle
come what may

Treat them not like the forever sole breadwinner
Appreciate them not into being quieter or
grimmer

Encourage them to be great dancers, chefs and
fashionistas
Therapists, caregivers, teachers and Modistas

For as a society, we must let them be
From my perspective, this is all I see

The divine feminine can truly be empowered
when
As a society, we empower our men.

Desert Rose

She dances in the desert afternoon

In the heat and hot winds,
In midst of the inferno and the sandstorm

The sands burn the soles of her feet
And words pierce a dagger through her young
heart

She has no possessions and not much to boast
about
She makes her own paths and follows her own
route
She comes from a community of dancers, who
have not much clout
They want nothing from the rich and the royals,
never go tout

She drinks from the cup of ecstasy, dances from
dawn to dusk
Oh, how they hated her free will! And titled her
'brusk'
She is uncouth, they all agreed

With not a care in the world, dancing on music
only she could hear
She fought for her freedom & her love, till her
body could no longer bear

She left behind some heartbroken souls when
she burned on her pyre
And the royals laughed and made merry thinking
they doused that fire

Well, she soon found a new place to dance and
love
Far from the inferno, in a new land up and above

She shared this cup of ecstasy with all who had
grieved
Continued to dance and continued to believe

The royals knew not what to do…
How can one possibly return from their pyre?!

They stood around, in utter disbelief
She is back to stir something deep in them, again
to their displease

She is a black rose in the desert, she does not
wither
And all who couldn't protect her dance in those
days are now tither

Mummy

The sun that lights up the darkest corners of my
heart and life
The woman who taught me what true,
unconditional love feels like
The warrior who taught me how to perfect each
strike

The chef whose homemade meals are to die for
The simplicity of her smile and her beautiful
eyes I adore
She is in my heart's heart, my very being's core

Staying away from her is the toughest part of
growing up
Not having her around often makes me go numb

Her comfort, whim and fancy are my number
one priority
Tears of joy and pride in her eyes, are all that I
want to see
Seeing her happy and fulfilled leaves me in a
state of glee

My Guru, my teacher and my best buddy
The anchor of my ship that always keeps me
steady
The foundation of my success, my role model
and my all-in-one remedy

Her hugs and calm words are what I call home,
Her voice is my heaven and that is all I call my
own

Longing

I long for something, in the core of my heart
I long for something, and it tears me apart
I long for something, from the very start
I long for something, a very important part

I long for something, a song or a piece of art
The song of the songbirds, a mouthful of an
apple tart

The ever-expanding universe and the wave of
the ocean
The vibrant colours of the flowers and butterflies
The never-ending bliss in emotions

I long for warmth and peace in each face
A lovely smile, a pepped-up pace
Spring and summer all year long
The lovers walking together, singing a love song
No hatred, no divide, no voices like shard
Difficult to explain, and finding it is hard

I yearn for the sun's warm glow and light
I long for the tiny ant's focus and the whale
shark's might

I long for every child's future to be bright
The nature left as wilderness, a pretty sight

I long for something, every day and every night
I long for my higher self and hope I do her right

VIBGYOR

This one is for the people who flow like the river
The ones who make the proud colors of the
rainbow

Those who don't fit into the 0's & 1's of the
binary
Those whose love is not bound to their partner
and their sexuality

To those who battle every day for basic human
rights
To those whose normal days can seem like a
fight

A fight against patriarchy and the binary
division mentality
A fight against closed minded colleagues,
friends and family

To those who deal with treacherous and masked
partners
To those who work tirelessly and support they
garner

To those setting boundaries for their self-respect
To those taking a stand to do and not regret

To those alienated by their community
To those not fitting into the ideals of the society

To those walking with their head held high
To those masking their grief with smiles

To all of you I send hugs and high-fives!
Continue doing what you are doing, you are
absolutely right

Eyes

Her eyes lure me into a world unknown
I can't wait to explore it

Her eyes, seem like they contain all the beauty
of the universe in them

Dark Blue, starry, shiny and deep
I just can't stop thinking about them..
They take me to a different realm

They contain all the love in world, too much for
me to grasp

Those big eyes, shaped like a fish from some
lore
Intense, coddling and mysterious

She looks right into my soul, recognizes my very
being
She looks angry or intense sometimes…but
never mean

She stares back at me, as I can't take my eyes off
of her
She smiles back (did she?)… and I can't stop
looking at her

I want to look at her eyes all day and get lost in
them
I want her to look at me, with compassion in
them

My love attaining its highest peak and
transforming into devotion

Like a devout I keep looking in them,
Her eyes lure me into a world unknown

Friends

It is rare to find the 'solid ones'

Your soul tribe
Your forever confidante
Your platonic lover and
Your fun therapist

You can go days, even months without speaking
to each other
Yet when you meet again, it seems like barely a
moment has passed

They are your family, your comfort
They understand you better than anyone else in
the world
Always your shoulder to cry on
Your place when you feel like you don't belong

You laugh and wail together
Celebrate and fail together
You have grown up together and seen each other
flourish
Your personality and your thoughts they nourish

No topic is off the charts
Aliens, spirituality, health or a broken heart
You enjoy scrumptious food together and
appreciate some art
Binge watch reality TV, head to the bar

You are at different stages in life
Some single, some parents and some super
successful
Some are juggling their daily chores
The others are off finding themselves in nature
Yet you miss all of them alike, wish them all the
best for their life

Living far away from your friends sucks for sure
You miss their voice, their hugs and their quirks
You aren't always around for birthdays or
vacays
But you are thankful to have their presence in
your life

Your confidante, therapist and soul tribe

The Forest

In a mystical forest, where the canopy stops the
sunlight

Blue butterflies, fuchsia flowers
Green blades of grass, white waterlilies in the
pond
The muffled sounds of a waterfall nearby

The breeze feels cool and the sounds of the
forest fall like music on the ears
Songs of sound birds and the occasional croak of
the toad
Everything around feels magical and the trees
are engulfed in a faint gold like glitter

Rustling of leaves and the moist ground
Feels like my very feet are getting cuddles and
caresses
There's a deer family at a distance
The fawn a beautiful golden brown, looks at me
with a seeming curiosity

The forest gets prettier as I walk on by
Closer to the waterfall, the canopy thins

Shrubs and herbs grow in abundance
Pink clouds dancing overhead

The waterfall, white as milk, flows on
The water, cold to touch, is perfect for satiating
my thirst

The wood creatures watch as I stand there,
taking in this forest's surreal beauty

It is ….. a mystical forest indeed

Alt Real.ity

What if I had turned left that day…
On the road, in the rain

I wonder what it would have been like if I chose
to attend that other university?

Maybe a different career path,
A different set of friends
A different geography to study and work in,
A different academic trend

What if you had chosen me too..
And put up a brave fight
What if we had worked through our issues
Would it have been a better sight?

What if I chose to travel more
And meet many new faces
What if I became a full-time volunteer
And opted out of these sheep and rat races

What would happen if I changed my smallest of
decisions
To eat in a different restaurant or go for a stroll
in a different direction

Am I bound by destiny…like an invisible
thread?
Or am I solely responsible for the roads that I
tread?

I've made millions of choices so far in the game
I wonder if others get overwhelmed by the
same?

"You can be anything!" they exclaimed when I
was a child
Seeing where I landed, just seems pretty wild

Out of all the possibilities that existed
How exactly has this one persisted

It's baffling that in this world I could have been
anywhere, or anyone it seems
But I am me. And I'm right here…….a part of it
was meant to be….or so I feel

Dichotomy

There is a clear dichotomy
In the dance of democracy

Be it the west or the far east
With each side playing the victim and making
the other beast

And they dance beautifully in this dance of
deceit
Of right and wrong, victory and defeat

Hiding their wrongs and harping on the others'
Crying out wolf to everyone who bothers

What is it that the democracy really entails?
Isn't it true that for one to succeed, the other
must fail

'Rule of the majority' is the basic foundational
principal
Doesn't divide and rule then appear as the
beaconed signal?

What does the populace really want?
What is their grief, their worry, their haunt?

For choosing one side is the call of the time
You press the voting button, and hear that
distinct chime

For we know not the future of this dynamism,
this race
But to bring any changes to this scene,
We must continue to vote, even with a grimace

India

There is a state, with saffron and green
Tied together with a sacred white thread

The state is full of lush greens
Breathtaking waterfalls, pillars and beams
Vast desert and awe-inspiring mountains

Home to a history of grandeur and opulence
Strength, bravery and non-violent resistance

Foods made with a myriad of spices
The flavor, aroma and the color entices

People of varied races, castes and religions
Stay together peacefully in all the regions

The origin of zero and chess
Innumerable dance forms and musical
instruments to express

Architectural marvels and the Ranthambore
Tigers
Crown made of Himalayas and flowing mighty
rivers

An ocean to our name and loving Indie
elephants
The peacock-our pride and the biodiversity
enchants

The birthplace of ancient sciences like Yoga and
Ayurveda
The land of folklore and stories that bring us
together

My heart beats for you….India
Thank you for being my motherland

Fairyland

I am in fairyland

The angels and fairies gather around me
They dance sing and make merry
My mom is there serving some sweets
The weather is just perfect, no rain or shine

Everywhere I look there are piles of clouds
I can jump in them and float around
Everything that touches my skin is silk
It's perfect! I think to myself

There is gold and diamonds and a dump of
dresses
There is a myriad of colours, Angels have long
tresses

There is no stress and no worry
And absolutely no need to hurry
It's indeed a heavenly vacation
Where there is no need for me to have any
vocation

I can sing and dance freely like no one is
watching
We communicate through smiles, there needn't
be any talking

What's that horrible sound?
A vague thought crosses my mind
Wake up Beta it's Monday! Says my mom being
kind

Oh well, fairyland, I'm glad I went
Time to get back to the reality my friend

Technology

The reason that I am a poet, is you
I can talk to my sister who's sitting in the US,
thanks to you

I can swipe marriage prospects right and left,
thanks to you
I can move around freely, without carrying cash,
thanks to you

Flight tickets? No print needed, thanks to you
No bulky cameras or lenses, that is all you

I can job hunt and earn a living, wearing
pyjamas in my room cuz you're the real OG,
that's right-you!

The latest movies, to my high-school binge
series are at my fingertips- thanks to you
I can hear every song till I'm sick of it-Thank
you

Suddenly, the ideal body type is the
photoshopped IG model and the tiktok
influencer-thanks to you

The world has turned a lot more plastic-thanks
to you

People are always busy and barely productive-
that's all on you
Always looking for the perfect love; making no
real connections-thanks to you

Everyone has hundreds of friends, but sit in their
room lonely, thanks to you
For people have many friends and innumerable
woes, thanks to you

Delving Deeper

There is a whole world inside you, believe me

It contains an entire universe

It has planets and stardust, and dimensions
unknown
Some psychedelics may help you get there,
some people have sworn

The journey inwards is more treacherous than
any other
If you are cemented in your ego, don't even
bother

You can lose yourself completely, in the realm
inside
That is what has been said by the sages and the
wise

You can find immense peace or your childhood's
monster
All your negative feelings and fears that you
harbour

It is still something that I suggest you do
Take the help of a therapist or a Guru

The place inside might not be wonderland
But it will be worth the journey, believe me

Love

It feels like the strength of a hundred warriors
You can fight the world with your person by
your side
Your heart fills up with magic, merely by
looking into their eyes

Their smile makes you go weak in the knees,
One good date making you smile for days or
even weeks!

You grin at their flaws and imperfections
Their voice, their pet phrases and even
intonations

Their skin feels like silk, their eyes like the
ocean
The constant yearning for their voice and
attention.
The way they treat you, their care and affection
The way they single handedly can change your
life's direction

The bittersweet potion of love, that only the
brave enjoy
On the other hand, for some, it seems like a
mere delusion

In the most nascent form it nurtures and protects,
At the height of ecstasy, can turn into devotion

The simplest yet the most complicated feeling
known to man
It is what makes life worth living
Gives you the happiness, no luxury of life can

Heaven

Does it exist? I do not know

I've heard from the religious leaders
And some religious text readers
That it is a place too great to attain
Beauties, riches and comforts that can't be
explained

No one knows where it is located
Above us apparently, but what if the earth's axis
rotated?

I know not of a world in the afterlife

But I see what god gave us here on earth
Nature where of beauty there is no dearth

There is abundant food, peace, fruits and riches

What if we are all angels? And truly living, in
someone's heaven

PCOD

So I have this thing, it's called PCOD

What is it? you ask
Well it goes a little like this..

In my mind there is a constant chitter-chatter
The anxiety goes pitter-patter
No amount of exercise seems to make my
tummy flatter!
I eat so less! Well it does not matter
Every time I step on the scale, I only seem to get
fatter
My sleep schedule and routine all splatter
Creams, lotions, potions for the acne I slather
My body image, right in front of me in tatter

The intolerable period pain
The efforts to get my life together, in vain
The constant energy drain
Always foggy post meals, my poor brain
Yet a smile in front of the world I must maintain
With very few friends through the struggle I gain

Is she really that sick? Or does she feign?

Well I might have PCOD, but this is my life……
and my reign